Does
Grandma
Have a
Mustache?

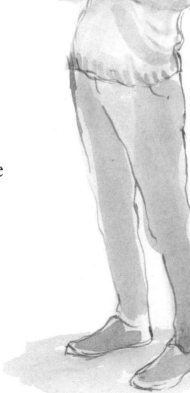

Rita Ann Fleming

Illustrated by Abigail Marble

Spring & Maple Books LLC
Jeffersonville, IN

Illustrations © 2015 Abigail Marble. abigailmarble.com

This book is a work of fiction. Names, characters, places and events are
products of the author's imagination or are used fictitiously. Any resemblance to
actual events, locations or persons, living or deceased, is purely coincidental.

First printing 2015

ISBN: 978-0-9864312-2-7
LCCN: 2015900443

ATTENTION CORPORATIONS, UNIVERSITIES, COLLEGES, AND
PROFESSIONAL ORGANIZATIONS: Quantity discounts are available on bulk
purchases of this book for educational, gift purposes, or as premiums for increasing
magazine subscriptions or renewals. Special books or book excerpts can also
be created to fit specific needs. For information, please contact Spring & Maple
Books LLC, 3209 Utica Pike, Jeffersonville, IN 47130; 502-552-6338.
DoesGrandmaHaveAMustache.com

DEDICATION

Thankful for
Geneva and Beatrice (Peach)

CONTENTS

Grandparents I

Please Read to Me

I'm not really tired.
It's too soon for bed.
I still need a snack.
I can't find my Ted.

This pillow is lumpy.
My jammies aren't on.
My night light is broken.
My blanket is gone.

But if you insist, Grandma,
Please tuck me in.
Our book's on the table.
Let reading begin!

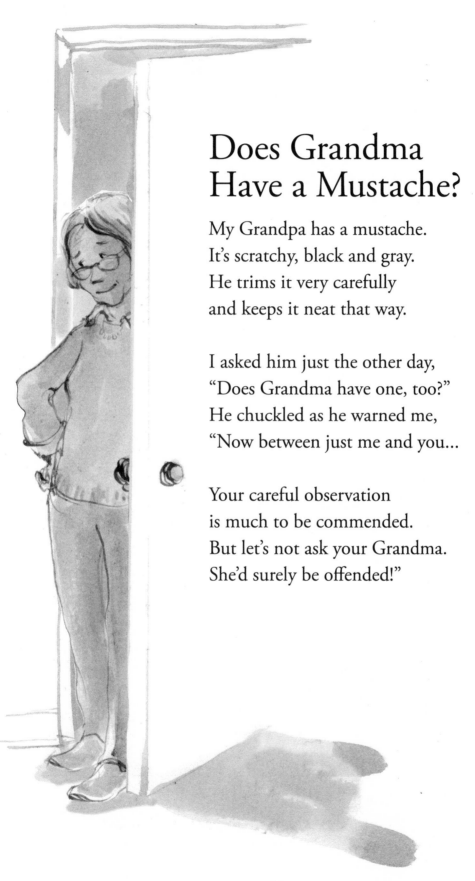

Does Grandma Have a Mustache?

My Grandpa has a mustache.
It's scratchy, black and gray.
He trims it very carefully
and keeps it neat that way.

I asked him just the other day,
"Does Grandma have one, too?"
He chuckled as he warned me,
"Now between just me and you...

Your careful observation
is much to be commended.
But let's not ask your Grandma.
She'd surely be offended!"

The Toy Trunk

Grandma spoke with great affection
of her attic toy collection.
We went upstairs. To our surprise
the trunk of dolls had come alive.

Thumbelina danced around.
Chatty Cathy made no sound.
Kewpie Doll met Howdie Doodie.
GI Joe was called to duty.

Baby First Steps walked a mile.
Raggedy Andy kept a smile.
Betsy Wetsy made a mess.
Barbie wore a brand new dress.

Lamb Chop looked for long lost sheep.
Hush Puppy said it's time to sleep.
We tucked them in and said goodnight.
Put down the lid. Turned off the light.

Fix-It Man

Broken lamp or ceiling fan,
flat tires on a neighbor's van,
if it's not working, Grandpa can
fix it—he's the Fix-It Man.

A falling fence or unhinged gate,
a cuckoo clock that sings too late,
a lawn mower in a sorry state,
a toaster that won't operate...

Toy airplane with a missing wing,
broken seat on playground swing,
a telephone that doesn't ring...
My Grandpa can fix anything!

Turn Off the TV

Let's have some fun.
Put your thinking cap on.
And turn off that TV.

Build Tinker Toys,
read Hardy Boys.
Play Old Maid with me.

Draw Etch-A-Sketch,
toss a ball, play catch.
Build a Battleship strategy.

Go run outside,
you'll seek, I'll hide.
Then we'll match in Memory.

Use sidewalk chalk,
take a long, long walk.
I think you'll agree with me—

When day is done
we'll have more fun
when we turn off the TV.

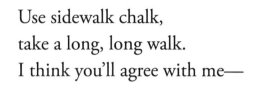

My Quarter

I found a shiny quarter
that I could not wait to spend.
I headed for the candy store
and took along a friend.

We looked at all the choices,
picked out a yummy treat.
We'd split it down the middle,
and both have half to eat.

But standing just in front of us
in line, all set to pay—
A little kid was crying as
he heard the cashier say:

"I'm sorry, you don't have enough
to buy this chocolate snack.
I need another quarter or
you'll have to put it back."

I whispered to my buddy,
"We'll come another day."
I gave the boy my quarter,
"Use this to help you pay."

My Grandma, right behind us, said,
"I hope you boys don't mind.
I'm going to buy two treats for you
because you were so kind."

CHAPTER TWO

Dilemmas

My Tattoo

I got a fake tattoo today.
I hope it doesn't fade away.
The skull and crossbones look so cool.
I want to show off at the pool.

It's summer time and getting hot.
A swim right now would hit the spot.
A hard decision to be made...
to jump right in or sit in shade.

I thought real hard and then debated.
Tattoos might be overrated.
I balanced both the loss and gain –
My tattoo's going down the drain!

Chewing Gum
No Longer Fun

This gum is so good,
  it's lasted all day
and I just can't bear
  to throw it away.
It's grape mixed with cherry,
  some peppermint, too.
I've added blueberry
  and wild honeydew.
The wad is delightful,
  but now I'm so glum.
It's bedtime and Dad says
  to toss out my gum.

Will it stick to the headboard?
  I think that it should,
but by morning it'll be hard
  and taste just like wood.
I think my best choice is
  to just try to keep
this gum in my mouth
  all night while I sleep.

The next morning...

I woke up at seven.
   I searched everywhere.
My gum? Oh, it's here.
   Firmly stuck in my hair.

My Toys Aren't So Bad

These are the worst toys
    a kid ever had!
They're juvenile, broken,
    outdated, and sad.
My floppy-eared bunny
    has worn off his tail.
I've lost several tracks
    and my train has derailed.

The wheels squeak a lot
    on my old Tonka Toys.
These trucks are intended
    for much younger boys.
Most of my board games
    are missing a part.
My red motorcycle
    refuses to start.

Wait! Mom has a sale planned
    for next Saturday!
She boxed up my toys,
    clearly marked "Give away!"
Well, maybe they're not,
    after all, quite so bad.
I'll still play a game with
    a missing doodad.

I do love my bunny.
        I'll find a new track.
I'll oil up the truck wheels.
        Please give them all back.
That used motorcycle
        still makes a loud zoom.
I don't want to live in
        a toyless bedroom!

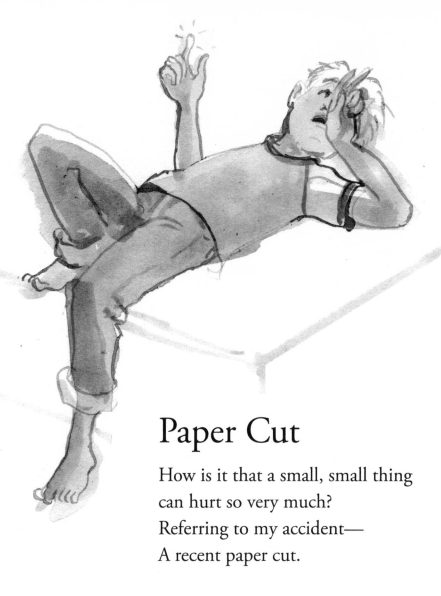

Paper Cut

How is it that a small, small thing
can hurt so very much?
Referring to my accident—
A recent paper cut.

My finger feels like it's on fire.
The pain has not subsided.
I simply cannot function
'til some first aid is provided.

No medicine is necessary
to treat this injury.
Only a chocolate ice cream cone
will end my misery.

Bear and Ted

My favorite pals are Bear and Ted.
I find them when I go to bed.
After all our poems are read
they share the same spot by my head.

One night my Bear was acting bad.
He really made my Ted quite mad.
The disagreement that they had
left me feeling mighty sad.

"Bear, you simply cannot fight.
Ted's on the left, you're on the right.
We'll all shake hands. Turn off the light.
Let's now be friends and say 'Good night.'"

Well-Warmed

I'm wearing four layers
of warm winter clothes.
All covered in fleece
from my head to my toes.

Don't ask me to ice skate
or throw a snow ball.
I've got so much on
that I can't move at all!

Long Way Back

We took a long, long walk today.
We got off track and went astray.
And turning back, to our dismay,
It's just as far the opposite way!

Double Dare

My friend put out a double dare.
He's pretty sure I'll take it.
"Jump across this puddle now,
I don't think you can make it."

I gave consideration
of what I'd gain or lose.
My Mom would be quite angry
if I ruined my brand new shoes.

I took a giant leap and jumped
that puddle free and clear,
but slipped after my landing
and fell right on my rear.

I don't back down when double-dared.
I had to take that chance.
My shoes remained quite clean, but now
I split my best school pants.

Can the Fairy Find Me?

I wiggled loose a tooth today.
It landed on the floor.
I picked it up. It's nothing new.
I've lost a few before.

But now I'm at my Grandma's,
supposed to spend the night.
Can the fairy find me
and get the address right?

My Grandma called the fairy,
"In case it seems unclear,
I live at Spring and Maple.
My grandson's staying here."

And sure enough the fairy came
just like my Grandma said.
She left a whole five dollars
near the pillow on my bed!

Fold-Up Bed

"May we sleep in the fold-up bed
   instead?"
"Sure you can," my Grandma said.
But while we napped
the springs had snapped
and we were trapped
in the fold-up bed.

Hair Not There

My Mom is mad I cut my hair.
Now there's a big bald spot right there.

My friend said we can glue it on.
No one would know the hair is gone.

"No," said Mom. "We can't have that.
I think you need to wear a hat."

My teacher said, "Young man, no way.
The hat must go and you will stay."

I'm at a loss for what to do.
Bad hair...no hat—I'll think this through.

I've thought it out. Seems like it's best to
go ahead and cut the rest.

Why an Appendix?

I know I need a liver,
intestines, spleen and heart.
But why was I created
with this extra body part?

My kidneys are essential.
Can't do without a brain.
But an optional appendix
is causing me such pain!

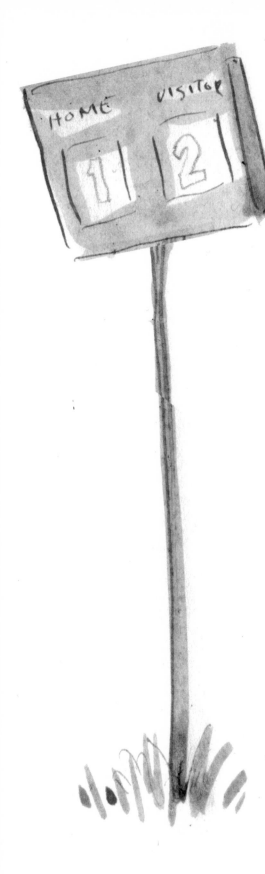

Soccer Score

"Please put me in coach!"
We need me in now.
Our team has to score
and I know just how.

My teammates were pumped.
The score was one-all.
The coach put me in
and I dribbled the ball.

I flew down the field.
I spun around quick.
The goal was in sight
and I gave a hard kick.

"My ball went right through,"
I yelled to my friend.
"That's great!" he said.
"But it's the other team's end!"

Just Can't Roll Right

I try to do a summersault
but never roll the way I ought.
Can't go straight, or left, or right,
I'm always stuck in plain hindsight!

CHAPTER THREE

Animals

Dad's Dog

Today I found a dog for you.
His coat is white. His eyes are blue.
His paws are big. His spots are black.
I throw a ball. He brings it back.

There're lots more tricks
that I can teach him.
So, I agree to let you keep him!

Feed the Fish

"I have for you
a little task.
Please feed the fish,"
my Grandma asked.

"Just a bit
is all it takes—
A little shake
of fish food flakes."

I shook the box
and fed all four.
They seemed to want
a little more.

Mike and Moby,
Fred and Finn
seemed grateful so,
I shook again.

If some is good
then more seems best.
I (cautiously)
dumped in the rest.

I figure fish
would know enough
to quit eating when
they're really stuffed.

But gosh, now
they're not moving much.
Their scaly skin
is cold to touch.

Mike and Moby,
Fred and Finn—
My overfeeding
did them in!

Kitten with Some Courage

I think we need a kitten
who'll become a fearless cat.
I know I saw two mice today
engaged in fierce combat.

They're fighting in my closet
and eating holes in clothes.
They might chew up my slippers
and start nibbling at my toes.

Mice with awesome appetites
could make a meal of Ted!
They'll pull apart my pillow
and leave droppings on my bed.

We don't need traps or bait or such
to rid us of this twosome.
A kitten with some courage
would be a good solution!

Gerry the Gerbil

Gerry, my gerbil, somehow got out.
His cage door is open.
   He's nowhere about.

My Grandma was tired,
   took time for a nap.
Woke up to find Gerry
   asleep in her lap.

"What is it?" she cried.
   "A rat? A raccoon?"
She screamed as she rose and
   ran out of the room.

Gerry was hurt, confused
   and enraged.
He sighed as he said
   "I'm better off caged."

Don't Be Rude
While at the Zoo

Grandma's new apartment
   is two blocks from the zoo.
We visit with the animals
   to get their point of view.

"Welcome to our house," they said.
   "It's nice to get together.
We welcome conversation
   so you can know us better.

We have a lot of visitors
   and offer some suggestions
for sensible responses
   to your frequently asked questions."

"Are you hiding in the winter?"
   we asked the grizzly bear.
"My cubs and I are sleeping
   in our warm and snuggly lair."

"Hey giraffe, why is it that
    your head is in the trees?"
"I have to stretch my neck so
    I can eat a lot of leaves."

The camel, once insulted, groaned,
    "Can't people understand?
I have to spit a lot because
    my mouth is full of sand."

The wild and bristly warthog said,
    "I try to be proactive.
When asked about my looks I say,
    'My friends find me attractive.'".

"I'm bigger than a lot of us,"
    admits the hippopotamus.
"You ask me why I eat so much.
    My appetite is bottomless."

We approached a few alpaca.
   "Do you mind the cooler weather?"
"Oh, not at all. We like the fall.
   Our wool is used for sweaters."

"Tortoise, must you move so slow?
   You're never in a hurry."
"I'm used to being last," he sighed.
   "It's not a cause to worry!"

"Come try this," the koala said.
   "You'll find it quite delicious."
"What is it?" we asked warily.
   "It's tasty eucalyptus."

We begged the anaconda,
   "Will you keep your distance please?
We fear that if you get too near
   you might give us a squeeze."

We met the giant cockroach.
   "Why do you tend to hiss?"
"It's just a scary noise I make
   but I'm not dangerous."

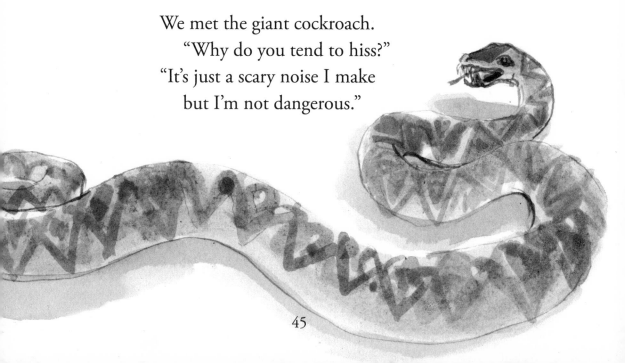

45

A wise owl flew down from his roost.
  "I now will ask you to
recall these common courtesies
    when coming to the zoo.

"Don't feed us things we shouldn't eat.
    Don't throw debris and dirt.
Don't call us some insulting names.
    Our feelings do get hurt.

"Remember this is our house,
    so please behave your best.
Don't be rude while at the zoo.
    You are, in fact, our guest."

Grandpa's Dog

My Grandpa has an old dog
who lies all day by his chair.
Except for when he sits to stretch
you'd hardly know he's there.

He doesn't seem to hear too well
when asked to fetch or stay.
But tell him that it's dinner time
he'll jump up right away!

Don't Blame the Bee!

I told my Mom, "Just wanted to see
if it really hurt when I stepped on a bee.
Bees don't look mean just flying around.
Their buzzing is really a most pleasant sound."

She said, quite alarmed, "Son, listen to me.
It will hurt quite badly to step on a bee."
But the kid next door said, "What?
    Are you scared to?
Go step on it now. I double dog dare you."

I took off my shoe and faced all my fears.
Stepped right on that bee and burst into tears.
"Don't blame the bee," Mom had to say.
"It's his way of trying to keep you away."

CHAPTER FOUR

Family

In the Middle

You'll find me in the middle,
stuck somewhere in-between
the oldest and the youngest.
I'm seldom heard or seen.

I'm squeezed between my sisters.
I'm neither big nor small.
Sometimes I do wonder if
I'm noticed much at all!

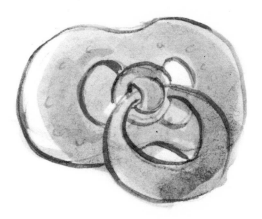

The Pacifier

It costs about a dollar
but is worth its weight in gold.
My mother bought one hundred
where the baby things are sold.

We've hidden them all over
the house and the basement too.
'Cause when the baby wants one
no substitute will do.

Some say we're quite indulgent.
We really should deny her.
But no one sleeps a wink without
the baby's pacifier.

No Peas, Please

"I've had it!" Mom said.
"Can't take any more.
I'm tired of you kids
throwing peas on the floor!"

"Now carrots I'll eat,"
said big sister Sue.
"Beets aren't so bad,
but these peas just won't do."

"They slide off my fork,"
I said with chagrin.
"I open my mouth, but
    few peas will go in."

"I'm warning you kids.
You know how to stop it!
No peas on the floor!"
(Now they go in our pocket!)

Vacation

We're going on vacation
   and I can hardly wait.
We packed the car, locked the door,
   and closed the backyard gate.
Then Dad said, "Just one minute.
   My wallet's still inside."
We turned around,
   he jumped right out,
   then we resumed our ride.

First,the baby started crying
   and threw up in the car.
Then, my hands got sticky
   while I ate a melted candy bar.
We drove about three hundred miles.
   My dad said "Halfway there!"
He hit a bump,
   the tire went flat,
   and we forgot the spare.

At quarter after seven
    we reached our destination.
The desk clerk said,
    "I'm sorry, but you have
    no reservation."
We finally found a hotel
    with towels that didn't match.
The sink was clogged,
    the window stuck,
    the door refused to latch.

We woke up early morning
    so Mom and Dad proposed,
"Let's go get a bite to eat."
    But the breakfast bar was closed.

The swimming pool had algae.
  The baby got heat rash.
My mom had lost her credit card
  and we were out of cash.

I must have eaten some bad food.
  My stomach felt all wrong.
We found a great amusement park.
  The lines were really long.
On Sunday night we headed home
  and drove through lousy weather.
But we agreed our trip was fine,
  because we were together!

Onesie

I'm helping get the baby dressed.
Me and Grandpa doing our best.
The socks and shoes—we're okay there.
Our problem's with the underwear.

It's a one-piece thing that must be snapped.
I fear she'll be forever trapped.
The sleeve is tight around her knee.
The neck hole's where the sleeve would be.

The snaps don't line up right, instead
they gather up atop her head.
Her feet are inches from her chin.
It's inside out and inside in.

The baby squirmed and got away.
She won't wear underwear today!

I'll Trade

The poet named Shel
had a sister to sell.
Here's offering up another.

I'll trade her for
two toys or more.
I'd much prefer a brother!

Baby Food

I'm helping feed the baby
'cause Mom is running late.
This stuff is indescribable
that's on her kiddie plate.

There's slimy, squishy spinach,
pureed peas and pears.
A bit of food goes in her mouth
but most of it she wears.

"Eat some more," I try to coax.
She throws her spoon instead.
I guess she's had enough, because
her dish is on her head.

"Not Me"

There's someone in our family
who's simply named "Not Me".
He wanders through our house a lot
with no identity.

He's blamed for all the mischief
if the culprit isn't clear.
We're sure it's him if milk is spilled
or cookies disappear.

And if a window's broken
no one will claim the ball,
'cause we know it's never one of us...
It's "Not Me" after all.

Cooking Class

My sister is in cooking class
to learn some new cuisine.
Since then, my Dad eats out a lot.
We kids are getting lean.

She usually burns the biscuits.
Her oatmeal tastes like grit.
Her waffles are just awful,
but her Pop Tarts are a hit.

Her popcorn ruins the microwave,
so we eat chips and dip.
Her Jell-o just stays juicy,
but she serves some good Cool Whip.

My Grandma's won blue ribbons
for all the things she bakes.
She's hopeful there'll be progress that
my sister slowly makes.

Just Kidding

Dear Mom and Dad,

We're having fun while you are gone.
We watch cartoons the whole day long.
For breakfast, I served six S'mores.
We see no point in doing chores.

Our baby sitter ran away.
She saw a mouse and wouldn't stay.
    (Told you!)
We bought a gym set for the yard
and charged it on your credit card.

Our cookout was a big success.
The firemen now know our address.
Today we cut the grass for you
and mowed the neighbors' flowers, too.

Last night my sister had a date.
She met some friends
    you'll REALLY hate.
Well, maybe I exaggerate.
Grandma let me stay up late.

We wrote this poem and
    had a snack.
Just kidding, Mom.
    Don't hurry back.

Love, Nick

Questions

"How come?" "What if?" "Who said?"
repeats Gary's little brother.
"His questions drive us crazy!"
we confided to his mother.

"Why is he so annoying?
Please explain this kid!
She smiled, "Well boys, he simply asks
the same things that you did."

CHAPTER FIVE

School

Science Fair

I found some tiny fishes
along a river bank.
Said, "Here's my science project."
and put them in a tank.

"I'm going to demonstrate," I said,
"just how they learn to swim.
I'll plot it on some charts and graphs.
I'm pretty sure I'll win."

While busy with my data,
recording in my logs,
right at the competition
my subjects became frogs.

They hopped on all the tables
and made a croaking noise.
And quickly, from the classroom,
ran all the girls and boys.

I'm proud of my achievement.
I won the science fair.
The kids were gone and then, I was
the only one left there!

Spelling Bee

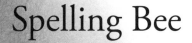

My sister studied hard
to win the spelling bee.
The hardest words, she says, are those
with "i" before an "e."

She knew of one exception—
the rule for "after c."
So she was right on target
when she spelled the word "receive."

But she forgot another rule—
when sounding like "long a."
If using "e" before the "i,"
as in neighborhood and weigh.

I'm Really Mad!

Don't get me started.
I'm already mad!
This is the worst day
that I've ever had!

I woke up too late
and rushed to get dressed.
My shoes didn't match.
My hair was a mess.

My oatmeal was cold.
The toast was too dry.
I spilled my hot chocolate
My eggs wouldn't fry!

I put on my coat.
The zipper was stuck.
It's started to rain.
I'm having no luck!

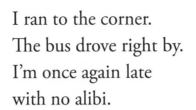

I ran to the corner.
The bus drove right by.
I'm once again late
with no alibi.

My teacher was angry.
My homework was lost.
I broke my retainer—
how much does it cost?

Recess was cancelled.
I don't get to play.
Boy, am I glad
that it's Friday today!

Sewing Class

My sister, after sewing class, said
"Try this shirt on, please.
I made it last week, just for you,
and need to hem the sleeves."

I put it on and clearly saw
six buttons lined up wrong.
The collar was turned inside out.
The shirt was much too long.

She wanted me to show it off
and wear it at my school.
Surprisingly, the kids all thought
my shirt was mighty cool!

Spelling Test

Next week I have a spelling test.
I'll try real hard to do my best.
But it's days away so now I'll play.
Won't worry about that spelling test.

In five days I have a spelling test.
I should study to do my best.
I sat. I tried, but it's nice outside.
Well, so much for that spelling test.

Three days away is my spelling test.
I just don't know if I'll do my best.
I'm down, depressed and need a rest
from the strain of that spelling test.

Today, an hour away, is my spelling test.
There's no way I'm going to do my best.
But my teacher is ill, so the substitute will
reschedule that dreaded spelling test.

So, a week from now is my spelling test.
I am determined to do my best.
I'll study now 'cause I see just how
I lucked out on my spelling test.

Contagious

Got the worst news in the world—
I'm paired at recess with a girl.
I better think of something quick.
I'm starting to feel really sick.

Excuse me, teacher. Listen please.
I'm coming down with some disease.
I have a sneeze, a cough, a chill.
Don't want to make a classmate ill.

We found this in the early stages,
before I'm terribly contagious.
I better see the nurse instead
and heal up in the sick room bed.

CHAPTER SIX

Adventure

Camping Trip

My friend and I decided
to camp outside all night.
My mom was apprehensive
but then said, "Well, all right."

My sister said, "I have some doubt
that you will stay out late.
You're such a scaredy-cat that you'll
be in the house by eight!"

We settled in our pup tent
and ate our nighttime snack.
My friend told me a story
before we hit the sack.

He then began a frightening tale
about some long lost boys.
He tried to scare me when he made
a weird, unnatural noise.

I started to get goose bumps.
I felt a little chill.
Then I sat up and challenged him—
"You're story isn't real."

I'm happy to report
my sister wasn't right.
I was brave and there I stayed
and camped all through the night!

Toasted

A perfect, toasted marshmallow
is really fun to cook.
The recipe is simple,
not found in any book.

First you find a bunch of sticks
and build them in a pile.
A grown-up lights the fire for you.
(This might take quite a while.)

Then load one stick with marshmallows
and wait for them to toast.
They'll turn to chunks of charcoal
if you hold them much too close.

When they've cooled a little bit
just pull them off the end.
They always taste much better if
you share them with a friend.

Mulberry Street

Let's hope to meet on Mulberry Street
and encounter a cat who wears a tall hat.
Learn what to do
if we find a WHO.

Feel a nice breeze through pink, tufted trees.
See socks on a fox, or Things from a box.
Express a strong wish
to count one or two fish.

Find eggs that are green, a Grinch who is mean,
a turtle too bold, or men growing old.
A big-hearted moose...
Thank you, Dr. Suess!

Escalators

I'm worried that the escalators
underneath have alligators
waiting with their big, sharp teeth
to pull the toes right off my feet.

(And if a gator sleeps awhile,
   he's wakened by a crocodile.)

I better step off really fast
This shopping trip may be my last.
I was relieved when Grandma said,
"How 'bout we take the stairs instead?"

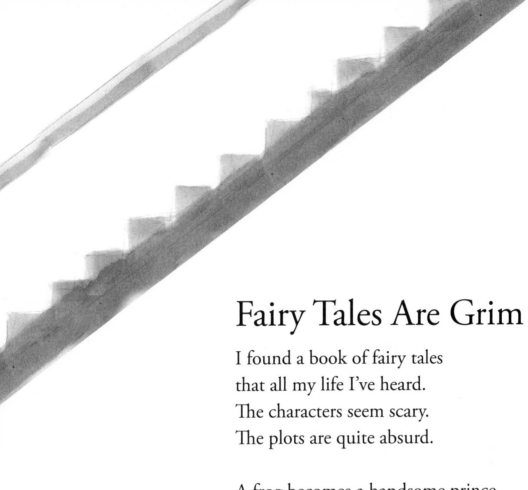

Fairy Tales Are Grim

I found a book of fairy tales
that all my life I've heard.
The characters seem scary.
The plots are quite absurd.

A frog becomes a handsome prince.
A boy buys magic beans
that grow into a giant stalk.
There's plotting, evil queens.

Some lost and lonely children
throw bread crumbs on their trail.
A wooden boy will grow his nose
with each deceptive tale.

Grandma's frightened by a wolf.
The hunter rushes in.
I'm starting to have nightmares
'cause these fairy tales are grim!

Abandon Ship!

We heard it first at Sunday brunch –
an order barked by Captain Crunch.
"Attention on the gravy boat!
We need all hands to keep afloat!

"Asparagus, adjust the sail.
Lash it to the lobster tail.
Chicken wings to man the oars,
seated on the dinner rolls.

"Navy beans, you'll be first mate.
Your mission is to navigate.
Potatoes need to keep their eyes
focused on the threatening skies.

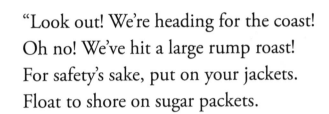

"Look out! We're heading for the coast!
Oh no! We've hit a large rump roast!
For safety's sake, put on your jackets.
Float to shore on sugar packets.

Abandon ship!
Looks like we're through!
Capsized in the Irish stew!"

CHAPTER SEVEN

Special Days

Bad Birthdays

It's not quite fair that I was born
December twenty-fifth,
because I get one combination
Christmas-birthday gift.

"I have a far worse birthday,"
explains my classmate Gary.
"Mine's celebrated on the
twenty-ninth of February!"

Where Are Those Easter Eggs?

With Grandma's new apartment
there's not a big backyard.
So hiding eggs on Easter
is particularly hard.

The bunny didn't disappoint.
He hid them all indoors—
under rugs, in the couch,
and on the upper floors.

We found eighteen or twenty,
but he hid twenty-four.
We searched all through the morning.
Could not find any more!

Easter eggs don't smell too good
when not refrigerated.
The odor from the furniture
was quite exaggerated!

My Grandma told the rabbit,
"While on your bunny trails,
next year we don't want real eggs,
just ones with plastic shells!"

Stuck Santa

He stopped on our roof,
got out of his sleigh.
But we were concerned –
how much does he weigh?

He's stuck in the chimney,
covered with soot.
All we could see was
one shiny black boot.

He said, "Well, it's tight,
but I thought I would try it."
Please, Santa, next year
go on a diet!

The Present

I know I should be grateful.
I hope things will get better.
But I was disappointed when
I got a V-necked sweater.

I thanked my Grandma nicely.
She said "Oh wait, there's more.
I thought about you when I saw this
on sale at the store."

And sure enough, she knew just what
a boy my age might like.
'Cause standing in the doorway
was a brand, new racing bike!

Thankful

I'm thankful on Thanksgiving.
It's time to celebrate
my family, friends, and happy times
that I appreciate.

I'm thankful for my parents
and sisters too (I guess).
Kudos to the substitute
who postponed the spelling test.

I'm grateful for my gerbil
(but sorry 'bout those fishes).
I truly love my Grandma
but could do without her kisses.

The science fair was super!
I'm happy that I won.
I appreciate my Saturdays
when all my homework's done.

I'm thankful for my Tonka Toys
and glad I kept my truck.
I'm hopeful Santa's lost some weight.
Next year he won't get stuck.

I'm thrilled with my new racing bike
to ride with all my friends.
And I can't wait 'til June the fifth.
That's when the school year ends.

Candy Bars
(Full Size, Please)

On Halloween we're at your door.
Please pass out what we're looking for!
Pay Day, Kit Kat, Snickers, Mars—
We like the full size candy bars.

We're okay with a Tootsie Pop.
A pack of gum is worth a stop.
We'll take a tiny Hershey kiss.
Fruit? Now there's a house we'll miss.

Fairies, vampire, goblins, ghosts—
Wwe surely know what we like most.
We'll come from near and come from far
to get a full size candy bar.

CHAPTER EIGHT

Grandparents II

Where's the Gray?

I noticed just the other day,
Grandma's hair seems much less gray.

I checked the front, the sides, the back.
I'm sure there's now a lot more black.

She sighed, "My dear, your vision's bad.
It's the head of hair I've always had!"

Grandma's Cookies

Mix the batter, roll the dough.
Lick the beaters, clean the bowl.
Frosted, sprinkled, sugar-dipped.
Oatmeal raisin, chocolate chipped.

Macaroons are soft and chewy.
Peanut fudge is sweet and gooey.
Grandma's cookies smell so good.
I'd eat fifty if I could!

Grandpa Snores

My Grandpa says he doesn't snore
but I know that's not right.
He snorts and sneezes, coughs and wheezes
in his sleep all night.

Grandma says she doesn't mind,
    she's lived with it for years.
But I have noticed when she sleeps
there's cotton in her ears!

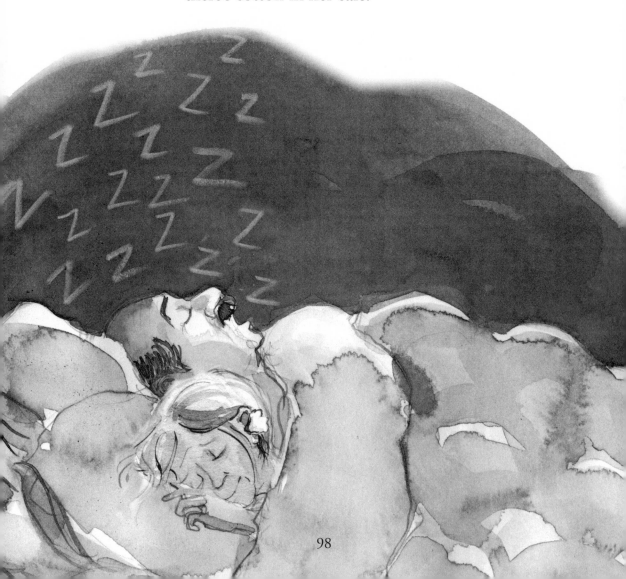

Eyes Where?

How can this be?
She can't see me.
I'm lingering behind.
Grandma said, "Indeed,
though I'm in the lead,
you're not too hard to find."

So I thought for a bit.
Said, "I don't quite get
when you are far ahead,
can you see where I go?"
She said, "Don't you know?
I have eyes in the back of my head!"

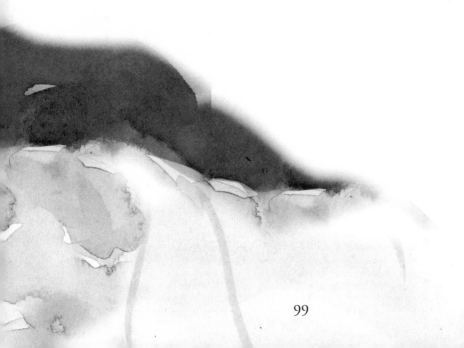

Grandma's Rulez

When Grandma asks a question
   and I respond to her,
I answer with a "Yes, Ma'am."
   To Grandpa with "Yes, Sir."

She has a list of other rules
   for things to say and do.
Her favorite phrases seem to be,
   "Excuse me, please, and thank you."

There's rules to put your toys away
   and wipe your dirty feet.
Help clean up the dishes.
   Put down the toilet seat.

Don't use embroidered guest towels
   or take too big a bite.
When here with your big sister
   don't argue, fuss, or fight.

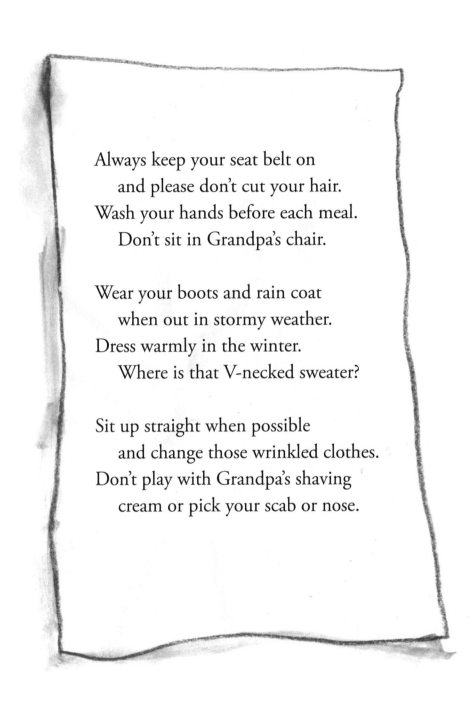

Always keep your seat belt on
    and please don't cut your hair.
Wash your hands before each meal.
    Don't sit in Grandpa's chair.

Wear your boots and rain coat
    when out in stormy weather.
Dress warmly in the winter.
    Where is that V-necked sweater?

Sit up straight when possible
    and change those wrinkled clothes.
Don't play with Grandpa's shaving
    cream or pick your scab or nose.

Don't scuff your shoes when walking
or overfeed the fishes.
And each and every day I'm here
give her hugs and kisses.

Not Scared Anymore

When I was real small
my Grandma took care
to look under my bed and be sure that there
were no monsters or dragons or ghosts anywhere
who might want to cause me
an awful nightmare.

But now that I'm big
I'm not scared any more.
Those monsters and dragons I can ignore.
But on your way out I'd like to ask for
you to leave on the night light ...
maybe open the door.

Grandma Reads to Me

My grandma called this morning.
She asked if it's all right
to pack my clothes and toothbrush
and stay with her all night.

When I get to my Grandma's
I choose what we will do.
There're cakes to bake and crafts to make.
We'll play a game or two.

When I'm tired I settle down
and say, "Please sit with me."
We pick the book and start to read
our favorite poetry.

I help her find her glasses.
We settle in our chair.
Grandma finds the book marked page
and reads to me and Bear.

We giggle at the verses
and pause from time to time
to look at illustrations
and find the words that rhyme.

I hope when I get older
and have a grandchild too,
We'll read these poems out loud
like me and Grandma do.

What's Next?

Did you like this book?
Would you care to look
for Volume Number Two?

"What's it called?" you ask.
It's "Did Grandpa's Dog Pass Gas?"
In a bookstore, soon, near you.

INDEX OF POEMS